Classic Recipes of
DENMARK

Classic Recipes of
DENMARK

TRADITIONAL FOOD AND COOKING
IN 25 AUTHENTIC DISHES

JUDITH H. DERN

CONSULTANT: JOHN NIELSEN

LORENZ BOOKS

This edition is published by
Lorenz Books,
an imprint of Anness Publishing Ltd,
Blaby Road, Wigston, LE18 4SE

www.lorenzbooks.com;
www.annesspublishing.com

If you like the images in this book and
would like to investigate using them for
publishing, promotions or advertising,
please visit our website
www.practicalpictures.com for more
information.

Publisher: Joanna Lorenz
Editor: Joanne Rippin & Helen Sudell
Designer: Nigel Partridge
Production Controller: Mai-Ling Collyer
Recipe Photography: William Lingwood

The image on the front cover is of Prawns
with Egg and Cucumber, page 32.

A CIP catalogue record for this book is
available from the British Library

PUBLISHER'S NOTE

Although the advice and information in this
book are believed to be accurate and true
at the time of going to press, neither the
authors nor the publisher can accept any
legal responsibility or liability for any errors
or omissions that may have been made nor
for any inaccuracies nor for any loss, harm
or injury that comes about from following
instructions or advice in this book.

PUBLISHER'S ACKNOWLEDGMENTS

The Publisher would like to thank the
following agencies for the use of their
images. iStockphoto: p6, Alamy: p13

COOK'S NOTES

Bracketed terms are intended for American
readers. For all recipes, quantities are given
in both metric and imperial measures and,
where appropriate, in standard cups and
spoons. Follow one set of measures, but
not a mixture, because they are not
interchangeable.

Standard spoon and cup measures are
level. 1 tsp = 5ml, 1 tbsp = 15ml, 1 cup =
250ml/8fl oz. Australian standard
tablespoons are 20ml. Australian readers
should use 3 tsp in place of 1 tbsp for
measuring small quantities.

American pints are 16fl oz/2 cups.
American readers should use 20fl oz/2.5
cups in place of 1 pint when measuring
liquids.

Electric oven temperatures in this book are
for conventional ovens. When using a fan
oven, the temperature will probably need to
be reduced by about 10–20°C/20–40°F.
Since ovens vary, you should check with
your manufacturer's instruction book for
guidance.

The nutritional analysis given for each
recipe is calculated per portion (i.e. serving
or item), unless otherwise stated. If the
recipe gives a range, such as Serves 4–6,
then the nutritional analysis will be for the
smaller portion size, i.e. 6 servings. The
analysis does not include optional
ingredients, such as salt added to taste.

Medium (US large) eggs are used unless
otherwise stated.

Contents

Introduction

Lying at the crossroads between continental Europe and Scandinavia, Denmark is a magical land of low-lying islands and a peninsula stretching out into the North Sea. Traditional Danish food is based around the natural bounty of this spectacular land, with fresh fish from the seas and rivers, and delicious pork and dairy products from the animals that graze on its fertile pastures. And with the Danes' deep-rooted sense of wellbeing, which manifests itself in a delight in dining with friends and family, you are certain of a warm welcome anywhere in Denmark.

Left: Traditional wooden fishing boats line the harbour wall in Copenhagen.

Danish Cuisine

Underlying the Danish attitude to good food is the concept of *hygge*. There is no literal translation for *hygge*. It is best described as mental and physical contentment, the security and warmth connected with good feelings about home and family, and includes eating and drinking with family and friends in a convivial atmosphere. Home is where the host or hostess can spread out a *koldt bord* (cold table) with assorted dishes (both

Above: Coffee and Danish pastries are often taken as a mid-morning break.

Below: A typical Danish breakfast consists of slices of rye bread, cheese and boiled eggs.

hot and cold), cheese, bread, schnapps, coffee and cakes. No guest will ever go hungry in a Danish household.

Danes start their day with bread, butter, sliced cheese, pickled herring and perhaps an egg. Lunch is normally a simple affair of *smørrebrød* (open sandwich) or a packed lunch if away from home. Dinner is the hot meal of the day, where the family gathers together. During the week it is generally one course, but soup, a main course and dessert (a pudding or cheese) is served at weekends.

Coffee and pastries generally follow a little later in the evening, with a small glass of liqueur. Late morning or afternoon coffee with a Danish pastry is a favourite work break.

The Danish open sandwich
Topped with lavish combinations of meat, fish, cheese, pâté, or even sliced new potatoes, with eye-catching garnishes that provide accents of flavour and texture, smørrebrød (literally "buttered bread") is a Danish original. It is eaten with a knife and fork and is enjoyed as a cold lunch on weekdays or on Saturday evenings with family and friends. When making smørrebrød there are few rules beyond buttering the bread with a lavish layer of salted butter, completely hiding the bread with the *pålæg* (topping), selecting harmonizing garnishes, and creating a sandwich with the highest quality ingredients.

Right: When serving open sandwiches for guests serve fish ones first, then meat.

Danish Food and Festivals

By law, public holidays fall on the same days as those of the Danish National Church. Other holidays mark historic dates or the seasonal swings from brilliant summer to deep winter darkness. Special foods are part of many celebrations.

New Year's Eve

Exchanging visits with family and friends to enjoy wine and small cakes is the traditional pastime as the year winds to a close. The wine is served with small cakes or biscuits such as mazarins, macaroons and vanilla rings. In the evening, families

Below: Macaroons are eaten on New Year's Eve.

enjoy a supper of baked or poached cod with potatoes, cauliflower, aquavit and beer.

Fastelavn

Once a period of fasting, *Fastelavn* (Shrovetide), on the Monday before Lent begins, has become a carnival-like event for children. They wake their parents by "beating" or tickling them with birch branches called *Fastelavnsris*, wear fancy costumes to school and feast on *Fastelavnsboller*, sweet, cream-filled Lenten buns, which they are given by their neighbours.

Easter

When the first snowdrops appear in spring, *Påske* (Easter) is just around the corner. Easter lasts from Wednesday to the following Monday, prompting lavish lunch parties, specially brewed beer and many glasses of aquavit. On Easter Sunday the main meal can include roast lamb, chicken or baked fish with spring vegetables. If the first asparagus has appeared, it is served as a special side dish.

Above: Lenten buns are given to children at Fastelavn.

Whitsun

"White Sunday", or Pentecost, is considered spring's official beginning when Danes rise early "to see the sun dance" after the long winter, and coffee must be ready on the table in the garden by 6 am. On the following Monday people go on country walks or bicycle rides to look for the first leaves appearing on the beech trees (the beech is Denmark's national tree). They celebrate with picnics or patio parties, and dine at *kroer*, where the season's first elver or eel, a speciality of these old inns, may be on the menu.

Midsummer Eve

Marking St Hansaften (St John's Eve) and the summer solstice, when daylight in the far north never ends, 23 June is celebrated with folk dancing, speeches, singing, bonfires, feasts and all-night parties. An effigy of a witch (a symbol of winter or death) is sometimes burnt in an ancient ritual condemning evil spirits forever to the fires of hell.

Mortensaften

An old family holiday, St Martin's Eve on 11 November celebrates the harvest and the legend that St Martin, reluctant to become a bishop, hid in a barn until some geese alerted the searchers to his hiding place. Perhaps as retribution, a fine meal with goose as the main course is served, followed by *æbleskiver* (doughnuts).

Christmas

In the weeks before *Julaften* (Christmas eve), houses are scrubbed, cakes and biscuits are prepared, farm animals are

Above: Christmas is a time to drink spiced wine with friends.

tended with extra care, sheaves of grain are put out to feed birds, the fir tree is cut or purchased, and gifts are gathered and wrapped.

On *Lille Julaften* (little Christmas Eve), on 23 December, friends and families gather for *glögg* (spiced wine) and æbleskiver dusted with icing sugar and served with jam. Christmas candles are lit and every house glows.

On Christmas Eve, families gather for three days of celebrations. Following church services, people enjoy a lavish

Christmas feast, featuring roast goose, duck or turkey, gravy, red cabbage, boiled potatoes, mashed parsnips or carrots, and always rice pudding for dessert. The *jule-nisse*, the elusive, red-capped, Christmas farm elf, is remembered with his own bowl of rice pudding to ensure good luck in the coming year. After dinner, the family sing carols, open presents and eat marzipan and sweet biscuits with coffee and liqueurs.

Classic Ingredients

Gardens, farms, forests, and the wide ocean have long supplied Danish cooks with a cornucopia of ingredients, and these staple products are still prized as the foundation of traditional home cooking today.

Meat, poultry and game

In peasant times, animals were raised on a small scale and so the traditional Danish diet included limited amounts of meat and poultry, which were primarily reserved for special occasions. Wild game, including hares, deer and small fowl, offered some year-round variety.

Below: Pickled herring features in many open sandwiches.

Times have changed since then and from the mid 1800s the farming of pigs, dairy cows and chickens has increased enormously. Although pork is now the most popular meat eaten in Denmark, other farmed meat products such as veal, lamb and beef also have their place on the weekly menu.

Fish and seafood

Surrounded by the sea, the Danes have always survived by fishing the prime waters around them. Coldwater fish such as herring, plaice, cod, Dover sole, halibut, flounder, salmon and prawns (shrimp), if not eaten fresh, were dried, salted or pickled using age-old preservation methods. As pork products took precedence in the Danish diet, fish lost some of its importance, though happily consumption is now rising again. Smoked and fresh eel, Greenland prawns (shrimp), gravlax (salt-cured salmon), cod, white flat fish, lumpfish roe and, of course, pickled herring remain the steadfast favourites.

Dairy

Used for cooking and flavouring, in savoury dishes as well as desserts and baking, the quality of Danish butter is superb. It is churned from cultured rather than sweet cream and has a low water content, making it ideal for pastry-making and baking.

The Danes' many regional and national cheeses have long added richness and flavour to their diet. Traditional cheeses range from soft to firm and include: *Samsø*, a mild, Swiss-style cheese named after the island where it originated; *Esrom*, a semi-soft, pungent cheese that grows stronger as it ages; *Havarti*, semi-firm with a network of tiny holes; a Danish version of Port Salut; and mellow-tasting *Thybo*, made with caraway seeds. Danes enjoy eating cheese on buttered rye bread for breakfast, and often include a cheese board at the end of a meal, but will rarely cook with cheese.

Right: Thybo ost, *a hard cheese from Thise Mejeri, on sale at a Copenhagen food market.*

Above: Danish cooks create a cherry sauce for many desserts.

Vegetables and herbs

The Danish garden overflows with vegetables. The well-fertilized soil, along with long summer days and a cool climate, create perfect growing conditions for cabbages, cucumbers, carrots, radishes, beetroot (beet), white and red onions, leeks, turnips and parsnips. Some vegetables – notably cucumbers, beetroot and red cabbage – are pickled for year-round use, while others, such as cabbages, parsnips, turnips and onions, are preserved in cold storage.

Danish cooks grow and use basic herbs in their cooking, either dried or fresh depending on the season. Parsley, dill, chives, thyme, marjoram, and creamed horseradish top the list of herbs used most often in traditional dishes.

Berries and fruits

From the first early strawberries to later raspberries, blueberries, currants, elderberries and gooseberries, soft fruits are eagerly anticipated and treasured. Grown in gardens as well as harvested wild, berries are used to make cordials, sauces for meat and poultry, desserts, fruit soups and fillings for Danish pastries or layer cakes. Lingonberries are a favourite turned into a sauce to serve with meat and poultry.

Apples, plums, pears and cherries are used in a variety of dishes, from apple cake to the traditional cherry sauce served with Christmas rice pudding. Rhubarb is another home-grown favourite and is a key ingredient in the Danish National Day Dessert *Grundlovsdessert* (see page 55).

Above: The Danes have many inventive potato dishes.

Potatoes

No Danish hot meal would be complete without potatoes. They were first planted in Denmark in 1642 in the Royal Botanical Garden, but not until 1719 did Danish farmers start cultivating them. Their popularity spread, even inspiring a dish based exclusively on the first small, new potatoes from the island of Samsø. Denmark's red- or brown-skinned potatoes are creamed, candied, mashed, boiled and made into warm or cold potato salads. A third of the total potato crop is eaten, a third processed as potato flour, and the rest become seed potatoes.

Mushrooms

In late summer and autumn, the Scandinavian woodlands burst with wild mushrooms. Trained from childhood to identify the best edible varieties – and to know where to find them – people head into the forests to forage for species such as ceps (porcini) and chanterelles and several kinds of truffle. Sliced and simply sautéed in butter and finished with cream, wild mushrooms accompany many pork or beef dishes. Traditional Danish cooks have always dried a percentage of their foraged mushrooms to use in the long winter months.

Below: Mushrooms of all kinds accompany many meat dishes.

Above: Home-made marzipan is used to make fruits and animals.

Marzipan

Finely ground almonds are blended with sugar and sometimes egg whites to make this sweet, pliable dough, which can be moulded into shapes and tinted with food colouring. Pastry chefs roll it into sleek sheets to mould over layer cakes or use as pastry fillings. At Christmas, families often spend an evening making small marzipan animals, decorated with dried fruit, to eat during the holidays.

Spices and seasonings

Danish cooks use many spices: a legacy of the nation's trading and seafaring history and French culinary influences. The US Virgin Islands in the Caribbean were once a Danish colony and served as a source for spices as well as brown sugar. White sugar, once an expensive ingredient, was used sparingly, and, as a consequence, most traditional Danish desserts are only slightly sweet.

The list of favourite spices includes ginger, cinnamon, cloves, cardamom and vanilla, plus caraway seeds for rye bread and for adding to cheeses. Dried mustard, white pepper, salt, distilled vinegar and cider vinegar are standard savoury seasonings.

Below: Danes use a variety of spices in their cooking.

Nordic Delights

Dip a spoon into a bowl of hot yellow pea soup, tuck into smoked pork, salt-cured salmon and pickled herring on an open sandwich, or enjoy cream-filled pastries with coffee, and you will be experiencing the same simple dishes that the Danes have been eating since medieval times. These historic dishes are still being served today because they taste fabulous and represent the very heart of traditional Nordic cooking – fresh, wholesome ingredients, lovingly cooked to perfection. The recipes that follow, honour this heritage with a collection of authentic dishes from across the country.

Left: Cured salmon is a classic Danish dish, often the centrepiece of the traditional koldt bord.

Yellow Pea Soup with Horseradish Cream
Gule Ærte med Peberrod Crème Fraîche

Serves 8

450g/1lb dried yellow peas, picked
  over
500g/1¼lb meaty ham bone or
  boneless pork shoulder
1 onion, chopped
3 carrots, sliced
3 medium leeks, sliced
10g/2 tsp dried thyme
175ml/6fl oz/¾ cup crème fraîche
  mixed with 15ml/1tbsp creamed
  horseradish
salt and ground white pepper
75ml/5 tbsp chopped fresh parsley,
  to garnish

1 Put the dried peas in a large, heavy pan and add cold water to cover. Leave to soak overnight.

2 Rinse the peas under cold running water. Return the peas to the pan and add 1.75 litres/3 pints/7½ cups water and the ham bone. Bring to the boil, skim off any foam, lower the heat, cover and simmer for 1 hour until the peas are almost tender.

3 Add the onion, carrots, leeks and thyme, and season to taste with salt and pepper. Cook for approximately 1 hour more, until the vegetables are tender.

4 Remove the ham bone, slice off any meat and return it to the soup. Correct the seasoning and serve sprinkled with parsley and a dollop of horseradish cream.

COOK'S TIP
If whole yellow peas are not available, this soup is equally delicious made with split yellow peas, or green peas, either whole or split.

Yellow pea soup is a wintertime favourite served throughout Scandinavia, with every country claiming ownership. A traditional country dish full of rib-sticking goodness, there are many variations depending on what vegetables are included (and what's in the pantry) and whether the soup is made with a ham bone or pork shoulder. Split peas speed up the process, but traditional Danish cooks favour whole peas.

Liver Pâté Leverpostej

1 Line one large (1.5 litre/2½ pint/6¼ cup) loaf tin (pan) or terrine, or two smaller loaf tins, with bacon. Lay the rashers across the tin, letting them drape over the edges, and reserving five rashers for later use.

2 Heat the oil in a small frying pan over a medium heat, and cook the onion, stirring, for 4–5 minutes until it becomes transparent. Leave to cool.

3 Preheat the oven to 180°C/350°F/Gas 4. Working in batches if necessary, put three of the reserved bacon rashers with all the remaining ingredients into a blender or food processor and pulse on low speed to blend thoroughly into a smooth, thick mixture.

4 Pour the liver mixture into the prepared loaf tin. Place the remaining two bacon rashers over the top of the pâté. Stand the loaf tin in the centre of a large, deep baking tin (pan) and pour in enough hot water to reach halfway up the sides of the loaf tin. Bake for 1½ to 2 hours.

5 Leave to cool, then chill the pâté in the tin for at least 2 hours before turning out. Run a knife around the edges first to loosen the pâté. Serve in slices on an open sandwich, or with wholegrain bread and pickled gherkins.

Serves 10–12

225g/8oz unsmoked streaky (fatty) bacon rashers (strips)
30ml/2 tbsp vegetable oil
1 medium onion, finely chopped
675g/1½lb pork livers, trimmed
225g/8oz minced (ground) pork
50g/2oz anchovy fillets
15ml/1 tbsp butter
250ml/8fl oz/1 cup whipping cream
3 eggs
2.5ml/½ tsp ground nutmeg
1.5ml/¼ tsp ground allspice
1.5ml/¼ tsp ground cloves
1.5ml/¼ tsp dried thyme
2.5ml/½ tsp dried marjoram
75ml/2½fl oz/⅓ cup sweet Madeira
salt and ground black pepper

Liver pâté is an absolute must on every formal buffet table in Denmark. While acceptable versions are available in the supermarket, nothing beats the rich, complex flavour of homemade liver pâté. It is traditionally made with pig's liver, but you can substitute the same quantity of chicken livers if they are easier to find.

Pickled Herring
Spegesild

Serves 4

400g/14oz salted herring fillets
250ml/8fl oz/1 cup wine vinegar
250ml/8fl oz/1 cup water
115g/4oz/½ cup sugar
1 carrot, thinly sliced
2 bay leaves
6cm/2½in fresh root ginger, peeled
and finely chopped
4cm/1½in fresh horseradish, peeled
and finely chopped
10ml/2 tsp mustard seeds
6 allspice berries
1.5ml/¼ tsp ground coriander
1 red onion, thinly sliced
dark rye bread, to serve
dill, to garnish

*No koldt bord would be
complete without several
kinds of marinated herring.
Dinners always begin with
herring and other fish
dishes, before changing
plates for the buffet's
various meat dishes,
salads and cheeses.*

1 To make the spiced pickled herring, rinse the fillets several times in cold water. Place in a bowl of cold water, cover and refrigerate overnight.

2 Combine the vinegar, water and sugar in a pan and bring to the boil. Boil, uncovered, for 10 minutes. Add the carrot, bay leaves, ginger, horseradish, mustard seeds, allspice and coriander; cook for another 10 minutes over a medium heat. Remove from the heat and cool.

3 Taste the herring for saltiness. If it is still too salty, rinse the fillets again. Otherwise, drain, cut into 2.5mm/1in pieces and place in a non-metallic bowl, layering them with onions. Pour the vinegar mixture over the herring and onions. Cover and refrigerate overnight or for up to four days before serving on dark rye bread, garnished with fresh dill.

Danish Caviar with Toast and Crème Fraîche
Stenbiderrogn på Riset Brød med Crème Fraîche

Serves 4

6 slices good white bread, crusts
  removed
100g/3¾oz lumpfish caviar
100ml/3½fl oz/scant ½ cup crème
  fraîche
½ red onion, thinly sliced
60ml/4 tbsp chopped fresh dill

*Trust the thrifty Danes to
devise inexpensive "caviar"
from the plentiful lumpfish
swimming in North Atlantic
waters. The lightly salted
black roe is a tasty
substitute for the real thing.
You don't have to be rich to
enjoy the mix of flavours and
textures in this simple,
classic presentation served
with toast wedges, sour
cream, thinly sliced red
onions and fresh dill.*

1 Lightly toast the bread and cut each slice into four triangles. Arrange
on a serving plate. Spoon the lumpfish caviar, crème fraîche and dill into
separate small bowls, and place on the serving plate. Arrange the red
onion on one corner of the plate.

2 Alternatively, spread each toast triangle with lumpfish caviar. Top with
a teaspoon of crème fraîche and a slice of red onion, and sprinkle with
chopped dill.

COOK'S TIP
Substitute red lumpfish caviar for the black variety, sour cream for the
crème fraîche, and chopped fresh basil leaves for the dill.

Jerusalem Artichokes au Gratin
Jordskokkegratin

Serves 4

250ml/8fl oz/1 cup sour cream
50ml/2fl oz/¼ cup single (light)
    cream
675g/1½ lb Jerusalem artichokes,
    coarsely chopped
40g/1½ oz/½ cup grated Danbo
    cheese
60ml/4 tbsp fresh breadcrumbs
salt

1 Preheat the oven to 190°C/375°F/Gas 5. Lightly grease an ovenproof dish. Stir together the sour cream and single cream in a mixing bowl and season with salt.

2 Add the Jerusalem artichokes to the cream and toss to coat evenly with the mixture. Spread the artichokes evenly over the bottom of the prepared dish.

3 Sprinkle with the cheese, then the breadcrumbs. Bake for about 30 minutes, until the cheese melts and the top is brown and bubbling.

COOK'S TIP
Danbo is a mellow yet flavoursome semi-hard cheese, but if you can't find it look for Elbo, Havarti, or use a good English Cheddar.

The Danes have adopted these somewhat overlooked vegetables. Jerusalem artichokes are not related to globe artichokes at all, but to the sunflower, which is why they're sometimes sold as "sunchokes". They have a delightful, nutty flavour and appealing crunch, but choose tubers that are firm and fresh looking, without wrinkles. Peel them before cooking if you wish, or just wash them well. This dish is a lovely accompaniment to roast meat or fried fish.

Braised Red Cabbage Rød Kål

Serves 6

1.3kg/3lb red cabbage
50ml/2fl oz/¼ cup distilled white
    vinegar
25g/1oz/2 tbsp butter
1 medium onion, finely chopped
2 tart apples, peeled, cored and
    thinly sliced
50g/2oz/¼ cup sugar
120ml/4fl oz/½ cup blackcurrant
    juice or jam
1.5ml/¼ tsp ground allspice
6 whole cloves
salt

Sweet, tangy red cabbage is a wintertime favourite in Denmark. Outstanding paired with roast pork, it is also the traditional accompaniment for the Christmas goose or duck. With its sweet, sour and fruity flavours and vivid violet colour, this vegetable dish looks as good as it tastes.

1 Remove the outer leaves and core of the cabbage and cut into quarters. Thinly chop or shred the cabbage, and place in a large pan. Add 120ml/4fl oz/½ cup water and the vinegar and bring to the boil. Reduce the heat, cover and simmer for 1 hour, stirring occasionally to prevent scorching.

2 Meanwhile, melt the butter in a large frying pan over a medium heat. Stir in the onion and apple and cook for 5–7 minutes until soft.

3 Stir the apples and onions into the cabbage with the sugar, blackcurrant juice or jam, allspice and cloves, and season with salt. Simmer gently for a further 1½ hours. Adjust the seasoning to taste before serving.

Cucumber Salad Agurkesalat

Serves 6

1 large cucumber, about 35cm/14in
  long
75ml/5 tbsp distilled white vinegar
25g/1oz/2 tbsp white sugar
45ml/3 tbsp chopped fresh dill
salt and ground white pepper

1 Cut the cucumber into 3mm/⅛in slices and place in a serving bowl.

2 Combine the vinegar, sugar and dill in a small bowl and season with salt and pepper. Pour the dressing over the cucumber slices and toss to coat evenly. Chill until ready to serve.

COOK'S TIP
This cucumber salad is served with all kinds of poached fish, especially salmon. The vinegar and sugar can also be mixed into 250ml/8fl oz/1 cup sour cream for a richer, cream-style dressing that goes well with fish cakes and fried fish.

Hothouse cucumbers grow luxuriantly under artificial light and help to dispel the darkness of long Scandinavian winters. As a result, the cucumber is a favourite food in Denmark. The dressing should be perfectly balanced between sweet and sour, with accents of fresh dill. It is important to make this salad shortly before you intend to serve it, so the cucumber retains its crispness and doesn't become soggy.

Marinated Herring in Sour Cream
Matjes Sild med Fløde Crème Fraîche

Makes 4

150ml/¼ pint/½ cup sour cream
2.5ml/½ tsp creamed horseradish
15ml/1 tbsp pickled beetroot (beet) juice
3 matjes herring, about 150g/5oz, cut into 2.5cm/1in squares
115g/4oz/½ cup pickled beetroot (beets), diced
250g/9oz/1 cup Cucumber Salad, drained and chopped
25g/1oz/2 tbsp salted butter, softened
2 slices rye bread
2 round (butterhead) lettuce leaves
2 hard-boiled eggs, sliced
4 parsley sprigs
salt and ground black pepper

1 Combine the sour cream, horseradish and beetroot juice in a mixing bowl. Stir in the herring, beetroot and cucumber salad; toss to coat evenly with the sour cream mixture. Season with salt and pepper and refrigerate until needed.

2 To make the sandwiches, butter the bread to the edges, top with the lettuce leaves and cut each slice in half.

3 Leaving one curl of lettuce visible on each slice, spoon the herring salad over the lettuce. Arrange three slices of egg on each sandwich.

4 Season the sandwich with salt and pepper. Garnish each sandwich with a parsley sprig on top of the egg slices.

Fishermen have plied the seas around Denmark for centuries. Cod, plaice, mackerel and, of course, herring were plentiful in the cold waters of the Baltic Sea, North Sea and the Kattegat Straits between Jutland and Sweden. Silvery herring became a staple in the Danish diet, and the fat, young, reddish-coloured fish called matjes were especially prized for their flavour. They are perfect for creating open sandwiches.

Smoked Salmon with Dill and Lemon
Røget Laks på Franskbrød

1 First make the mustard sauce. In a small bowl, mix together the vinegar, sugar, mustard, egg yolk (if using) and oil. Stir in 7.5ml/1½ tsp chopped dill, and season.

2 Butter the slices of bread to the edges, top with the lettuce leaves and cut each slice in half. Leaving one curl of lettuce visible on each slice, arrange a slice of salmon on each sandwich, folding or rolling the edges to fit.

3 Spoon 5ml/1 tsp mustard sauce down the middle of each sandwich. Cut each lemon slice in half, twist and place in the middle of the salmon. Place a dill sprig on top of each lemon twist.

COOK'S TIP
A layer of thinly sliced cucumber can be substituted for the lettuce leaves, if preferred.

Makes 4
25g/1oz/2 tbsp salted butter, softened
2 slices crusty white bread
2 round (butterhead) lettuce leaves
4 (100g/3–4 oz) slices smoked salmon
2 lemon slices
4 dill sprigs

For the mustard sauce
15ml/1 tbsp distilled white vinegar
25g/1oz/2 tbsp sugar
90ml/6 tbsp Dijon mustard
1 egg yolk (optional)
50ml/2fl oz/¼ cup vegetable oil
7.5ml/1½ tsp chopped fresh dill
salt and ground black pepper

Smoked salmon is a delicacy in Denmark. Now primarily farm-raised in Norway or Scotland, thin slices of the succulent pink fish are a favourite smørrebrød *topping. So as not to compete with the salmon's rich flavour, crusty white bread, or what Danes call* franskbrød, *is the preferred choice for this* smørrebrød. *The crusts are left on the bread, and a drizzle of mustard sauce with dill and lemon slices are the traditional garnishes.*

Prawns with Egg and Cucumber
Rejemad med Æg og Agurkesalat

Makes 4

25g/1oz/2 tbsp salted butter, softened
2 slices crusty white bread
2 round (butterhead) lettuce leaves
2 hard-boiled eggs, sliced
300g/11oz/2 cups small cooked prawns (shrimp)
mayonnaise
4 dill sprigs
8 cucumber slices
4 lemon slices

1 Butter the slices of bread to the edges, top with the lettuce leaves and cut each slice in half. Place 3 slices of egg toward the top of each lettuce leaf, leaving the top curl visible. Divide the prawns among the sandwiches and arrange them over the rest of the lettuce, partly covering the egg slices.

2 To garnish, top the prawns with a spoonful of mayonnaise and place a dill sprig in the centre of the mayonnaise.

3 Stack two cucumber slices with one lemon slice between them; cut the stack halfway across, and twist to form a curl. Repeat with the remaining cucumber and lemon. Place a cucumber-lemon twist on or beside each sandwich.

The icy waters around Greenland, a Danish province since the Viking era, are the preferred source for the sweet, wild prawns (shrimp) in this classic open sandwich. Heap the prawns over the lettuce or arrange them in orderly rows according to your style.

The Veterinarian's Evening Sandwich
Dyrlægens Natmad

Makes 4

25g/1oz/2 tbsp salted butter,
    softened
2 slices rye bread
small bunch watercress, thick stalks
    removed
8 slices Liver Pâté, 5mm/¼in thick
    (about 300g/11oz total weight)
8 thin slices deli pastrami (about
    115g/4oz total weight)
16 small sweet onion rings
4 tomato slices, seeded

For the beef aspic

250ml/8fl oz/1 cup boiling water
1 beef stock (bouillon) cube
1 sachet (15ml/1 tbsp) powdered
    gelatine
15ml/1 tbsp dry sherry

*This dish is named after a
Copenhagen veterinarian
who visited the Oskar
Davidsen smørrebrød
restaurant every day for this
very sandwich – morning
and evening.*

1 Make the beef aspic at least 2 hours before you need it. Pour the boiling water into a small bowl. Add the stock cube and gelatine, and stir until both are dissolved. Add the sherry. Pour the mixture into a small, shallow rectangular dish and chill for about 2 hours, until set.

2 To make the sandwiches, butter the bread to the edges and cut the slices in half. Arrange 8–10 watercress leaves on top of each piece of bread.

3 Place two slices of liver pâté on one half of the bread, and two slices of pastrami on the other half, cutting or folding them to fit.

4 Chop the beef aspic into 5mm/¼in cubes and place 4–5 cubes on top of the meats on each sandwich. Arrange four onion rings over the aspic cubes and garnish with a slice of tomato.

Pork Fillet with Crispy Onion Rings
Mørbrad Bøf med Bløde Løg

Makes 4

1 pork fillet (tenderloin), about
    400g/14oz–600g/1lb 6oz
25g/1oz/2 tbsp salted butter,
    softened
2 slices rye bread
2 leaves round (butterhead) lettuce
20ml/4 tsp remoulade
4 tomato slices
4 parsley sprigs

For the crispy onion rings

250ml/8fl oz/1 cup buttermilk
1 small onion, thinly sliced, rings
    separated
175g/6oz/1½ cups plain (all-
    purpose) flour
250ml/8fl oz/1 cup vegetable oil,
    for frying
salt and white pepper

1 Preheat oven to 190°C/375°F/Gas 5. Place the pork fillet on to a rack in a roasting pan. Season with salt and pepper. Place the pork in a preheated oven and cook until the meat is no longer pink and juices are clear, or the internal temperature reaches 70°C/160°F, about 1 hour. Allow the pork to rest for 15 minutes before slicing 16 slices about 5mm/¼ in thick.

2 Meanwhile, make the crispy onion rings. Pour the buttermilk into a bowl and season with salt and pepper. Add the onion rings, tossing to coat evenly, and leave to soak for about 10 minutes, then drain, discarding the buttermilk.

3 Place the flour in a shallow bowl. Dip the onion rings in the flour to coat them on all sides. Shake off any excess flour. Heat the oil in a frying pan. Fry the onion rings, in batches, over a medium-high heat until golden brown. Drain on kitchen paper.

4 Butter the slices of bread to the edges, top with the lettuce leaves and cut each slice in half. Arrange four pork slices on each sandwich. Arrange 5–6 crispy onion rings over the pork on each sandwich, and garnish with 5ml/1 tsp remoulade, a slice of tomato and a parsley sprig.

COOK'S TIPS

• Orange, cucumber or beetroot slices can also be used as garnishes.
• Cooked, sliced pork tenderloin can also be purchased in the deli department of many supermarkets.

Here, tender roast pork is garnished with two other Danish favourites – the much-loved remoulade, and delicious crispy onion rings – to make this traditional open sandwich.

Beef Tartare with Egg Yolk, Onion and Beetroot
Bøf Tartar med Æggeblomme, Løg og Rødbeder

1 Slice the fillet steak into very thin slices. You will find this easier if you first place the fillet in the freezer for 5–8 minutes first and use a very sharp knife.

2 Butter the slices of bread to the edges, and cut the slices in half. Arrange 8–10 watercress leaves in a fan shape at the top of each slice.

3 Place the beef slices on the bread, overlapping the watercress, layering or folding the slices as needed and extending over the bread.

4 Arrange two slices of beetroot on each sandwich and four onion rings over the beetroot. Carefully place an egg yolk on each sandwich, centring it in an onion ring to keep it in place. Sprinkle with capers.

COOK'S TIPS
• Separate the egg yolk when you need it. So there is less chance of it breaking, simply transfer the yolk from the eggshell onto the sandwich.
• If you prefer not to eat raw egg yolk, substitute it with hollandaise sauce, again placing it within an onion ring.

Makes 4
350g/12oz fillet steak (beef tenderloin)
25g/1oz/2 tbsp salted butter, softened
2 slices rye bread
32–40 watercress leaves
8 slices pickled beetroot (beet)
16 thin slices sweet onion
4 egg yolks
25ml/1½ tbsp capers

Raw meat may not be to everyone's taste, but beef tartare is a luxury for connoisseurs, and is a sophisticated dish presented on an open sandwich. Contrasting textures and flavours in the garnishes, plus the drama of a raw egg yolk balanced on the tender meat, give this smørrebrød extra flamboyance. Buy the best-quality well hung fillet steak (beef tenderloin) you can find.

Salt Cod with Mustard Sauce
Kogt Torsk med Sennep Sovs

Serves 4

800g/1¾lb dried salt cod, soaked,
   skin and bones removed
1 litre/1¾ pints/4 cups water
30ml/2 tbsp salt
1 onion, sliced
1 bay leaf
10 whole peppercorns
4 whole cloves
4 lemon slices
60ml/4 tbsp butter
2 hard-boiled eggs, chopped, and
   chopped parsley to garnish
boiled new potatoes and sliced
   pickled beetroot (beet), to serve

For the mustard sauce

15ml/1 tbsp distilled white vinegar
25g/1oz/2 tbsp sugar
90ml/6 tbsp Dijon mustard
1 egg yolk (optional)
50ml/2fl oz/¼ cup vegetable oil
7.5ml/1½ tsp chopped fresh dill
salt and ground black pepper

1 After the cod has been sufficiently soaked, cut it into 4–8 serving-size pieces, and set aside.

2 Fill a large pot with enough water to cover the fish and add the salt, onion, bay leaf, peppercorns, cloves and lemon slices.

3 Bring the stock to the boil, add the fish pieces, lower the heat, cover and simmer until the fish turns opaque and flakes easily with a fork, about 10 minutes.

4 For the mustard sauce, mix together the vinegar, sugar, mustard, egg yolk (if using) and oil. Stir in the chopped fresh dill and season to taste.

5 When the fish is cooked, remove the fish from the broth with a slotted spoon and divide the pieces evenly among four warmed serving plates.

6 Top each serving with 15ml/1 tbsp butter, and generously sprinkle with the chopped hard-boiled egg and parsley. Serve the fish with the mustard sauce, boiled new potatoes and pickled beetroot.

Mustard sauce is the traditional accompaniment for salmon, but Danes also enjoy it with this salt cod and with other fish dishes. You need to soak the salted fish in plenty of cold water for 48 hours, changing the water several times. After soaking, taste a small piece of the fish to test its salt content – thicker parts may need to be soaked longer. This dish is often served with boiled new potatoes, pickled beetroots (beets), and if desired, grated fresh horseradish for some added pungency.

Fish Cakes Fiskefrikadeller

1 Place the cod and salmon fillets in a shallow dish, and sprinkle with 15ml/1 tbsp salt to draw some of the moisture out. Leave the fish to rest for 10 minutes, then pat dry with kitchen paper.

2 Place the cod and salmon, with the smoked salmon, in a food processor. Add the onion, butter, eggs and flour and pulse until smooth; season with salt and pepper and spoon into a bowl.

3 Preheat the oven to 190°C/375°F/Gas 5. Lightly grease a 23 x 33cm/ 9 x 13in baking tray. With damp hands, form the fish mixture into 16 slightly flattened, round patties, and place them on the prepared tray.

4 Bake the fish ⌐ ∃ in the preheated oven for 30–35 minutes, until they are cooked through and lightly browned. Serve immediately.

COOK'S TIP
Danish remoulade has a mild, sweet-sour taste and is similar to tartar sauce. It is normally made with mayonnaise mixed with finely chopped cabbage, pickled cucumber, sugar and a hint of mustard. It can be bought ready made in many supermarkets.

VARIATIONS
Serve the fish cakes with mustard sauce instead of remoulade. Instead of baking they can be fried or grilled (broiled).

Serves 4
450g/1lb cod or plaice fillet
225g/8oz salmon fillet
175g/6oz smoked salmon
30ml/2 tbsp finely chopped onion
40g/1½oz/3 tbsp melted butter
3 eggs
25g/1oz/¼ cup plain (all-purpose)
   flour
salt and white pepper

Baked in the oven, fish cakes are a steadfast favourite throughout Denmark. Serve the fish cakes with remoulade, buttered potatoes and Cucumber Salad to make a complete supper.

Fried Salt Herring with Red Onion Compote
Stegt Sild med Rødløgs Kompot

Serves 4

8 salted herring fillets (about
    675g/1½lb total weight)
15g/3oz/1½ cups fine breadcrumbs
40g/1½oz/3 tbsp butter
2.5ml/½ tsp white pepper

For the red onion compote

675g/1½lb red onions, diced
75ml/2½fl oz/⅓ cup cider vinegar
350ml/12fl oz/1½ cups red wine
250ml/8fl oz/1 cup water
50ml/2fl oz/¼ cup honey
15ml/1 tbsp soft light brown sugar
10ml/2 tsp butter
salt and ground black pepper

1 Rinse the herring several times in cold water. Place in a bowl of cold water, cover and leave to soak overnight in the refrigerator.

2 Taste the herring for saltiness. If it is too salty, rinse the fillets again. Otherwise, drain, pat dry with kitchen paper and place on a plate.

3 To make the red onion compote, place the diced onion in a pan and add the vinegar and red wine. Bring to the boil and cook, uncovered, over a medium heat for about 30 minutes, stirring occasionally, until the liquid has evaporated. Stir in the water, honey, brown sugar and butter, and season with salt and pepper. Cook for a further 15 minutes, stirring occasionally, until reduced and thick. Cover and keep warm until needed.

4 Place the breadcrumbs in a shallow dish and dip the herring fillets into the crumbs to coat both sides evenly. Sprinkle with pepper.

5 Melt the butter in a large frying pan over a medium-high heat. Fry the herring fillets, in batches if necessary, turning once, for about 4 minutes on each side, until the coating is golden brown and the fish flakes easily with a fork. Remove the fish from the pan, drain on kitchen paper, and keep warm until all the fillets are cooked.

6 Divide the fillets between four serving plates. Spoon the red onion compote over the fish and serve immediately.

By the 12th century, salt herring was a staple food throughout Scandinavia. Although salt was rare and costly in medieval times, it was worth the expense to preserve the seasonal shoals of herring. Even though there are now other ways of preserving herring, the Danes have retained a taste for salted fish.

Roast Pork, Crackling and Glazed Potatoes
Flæskesteg med Svær og Sukkerbrunede Kartofler

1 Preheat the oven to 200°C/400°F/Gas 6. Use a sharp knife to score the pork skin with diagonal cuts. Rub the rind with the salt, pepper and mustard powder. Push the cloves and bay leaves into the skin. Place the pork loin, skin side up, on a rack in a roasting pan and cook for about 1 hour, until the skin is crisp and golden. Pour the water into the bottom of the roasting pan and cook for a further 30 minutes.

2 Boil the potatoes in salted water for 15–20 minutes, or until soft. Drain, peel and keep warm. Melt the sugar in a frying pan over a low heat until it turns light brown. Add the potatoes and butter, stirring to coat the potatoes, and cook for about 6–8 minutes, until the potatoes are a rich golden brown. Keep warm.

3 To cook the apples, bring the water to the boil and stir in the brown sugar. Add the lemon juice and apple halves, lower the heat and poach until the apples are just tender. Remove the apples from the pan. Spoon 7.5ml/1½ tsp redcurrant jelly onto each apple half and keep warm.

4 When the pork is cooked, transfer it to a serving dish and leave it in a warm place to rest for 15 minutes before carving. Meanwhile, make the gravy; transfer the roasting pan juices into a pan and reduce over a medium heat. Whisk in a little cream if you wish, and season with salt and pepper to taste.

5 Remove the crackling from the pork, and serve it separately. Serve the pork with the gravy, caramelized potatoes and poached apple halves.

Pork is the favourite meat in Denmark, and roast pork with golden crackling is a much-loved dish, especially during winter. For this recipe, select a bone-in pork loin with the skin left on for the crackling.

Serves 8–10

1 bone-in pork loin, weighing about 2.25kg/5lb
10ml/2 tsp mustard powder
15 whole cloves
2 bay leaves
900ml/1½ pints/3¾ cups water
175ml/6fl oz/¾ cup single (light) cream (optional)
salt and white pepper

For the glazed potatoes

900g/2lb small potatoes
50g/2oz/¼ cup caster (superfine) sugar
65g/2½ oz/5 tbsp butter

For the apples with redcurrant jelly

750ml/1¼ pints/3 cups water
115g/4oz/generous ½ cup soft light brown sugar
5ml/1 tsp lemon juice
4–5 tart apples, peeled, cored and halved
60–75ml/4–5 tbsp redcurrant jelly

Danish Meatballs Frikadeller

1 In a small bowl, beat the eggs well. In a separate, larger bowl, mix the minced veal, minced pork, breadcrumbs and chopped onion together until well blended. Mix in the beaten egg. You might find it easier to use your hands rather than a spoon to blend the ingredients properly.

2 Add the milk, salt and pepper to the bowl and continue mixing until all the ingredients are thoroughly blended to make a soft, moist mixture. Refrigerate the mixture for 15–30 minutes, or until you are ready to cook the meatballs; this will help you to shape it into balls.

3 Melt the butter in a large frying pan over a medium heat. Use two spoons to form 16–20 oval patties about 4cm/1½in across: scoop the meat mixture with one spoon and use the second to slide the patty into the pan.

4 Cook the meatballs for 8–10 minutes, in batches of four or five if necessary, turning once, until the patties are golden brown. Cut one to check that the meat is not pink in the centre. Remove the cooked meatballs from the pan and drain on kitchen paper. Keep warm until all the meatballs are cooked. Serve immediately.

Serves 4

2 eggs
225g/8oz minced (ground) veal
225g/8oz minced (ground) pork
25g/1oz/½ cup fine breadcrumbs
40g/1½oz/½ cup finely chopped
  onion
250ml/8fl oz/1 cup milk
75g/3oz/5 tbsp butter
salt and ground black pepper

COOK'S TIP

Make a double batch of meatballs and freeze them, uncooked, for up to three months. You can also freeze them after they are fried, and then reheat them in the oven. When rolled into much smaller balls, the meatballs are often served at parties as finger food, with pickles.

Some say this is the national dish of Denmark. Traditionally served in Danish homes at least once a week, it's a recipe every cook knows in two or three versions. When eaten for the evening meal, frikadeller are served with gravy, boiled potatoes and red cabbage or sliced dill pickles.

Beef Patties with Onions and Fried Egg
Hakkebøf med Bløde Løg

Serves 4

450g/1lb lean minced (ground) beef
45ml/3 tbsp breadcrumbs
20g/¾oz/¼ cup finely chopped
    onions
5 eggs
15g/½oz/¼ cup chopped parsley
120ml/4fl oz/½ cup milk
65g/2½oz/5 tbsp butter
3 medium onions, sliced
salt and ground black pepper

1 Put the beef in a mixing bowl, add the breadcrumbs, chopped onion, one egg and parsley and mix well. Gradually stir in the milk until thoroughly blended to make a soft, moist mixture. Season with salt and pepper. Refrigerate for 15–30 minutes.

2 Melt 40g/1½oz/3 tbsp of the butter in a pan over a medium heat. Divide the meat mixture into four and form rounded patties. Place in the pan and cook for 8–10 minutes, turning once, until browned. Remove from the pan and keep warm.

3 Melt the remaining butter in the pan, add the sliced onions and cook for 6–8 minutes, until soft and golden. When the onions are ready, fry the eggs in a little hot oil in a separate pan.

4 To serve, place the patties on four serving plates and top each with a spoonful of cooked onions. Place a fried egg on the onions and serve immediately on warmed plates.

Fried beef patties are a very old, traditional Danish dish, a workers' meal still enjoyed today all around the country. Most often eaten at lunchtime, the patties are served with buttered flat bread and pickled red cabbage or gherkins.

Venison Tenderloins with Cherry Sauce
Dyrefilet med kirsebær sovs

1 Preheat the oven to 230°C/450°F/Gas 8. Tie the venison at 2.5cm/1in intervals with fine string to hold its shape while roasting. Sprinkle with salt and pepper, and spread with butter. Place on a rack in a shallow roasting pan, and pour in the water. Cook in the hot oven for 20 minutes to brown the surface.

2 Lower the heat to 180°C/350°F/Gas 4. Continue to cook the tenderloin, basting at intervals with the pan juices, for a further 1¼ hours, until barely pink in the centre (65°C/150°F on a meat thermometer). Leave the meat in a warm place to rest for 10 minutes before slicing.

3 Meanwhile, to make the sauce, bring the cherry juice to the boil in a pan over a medium-high heat. Whisk together the water and cornflour in a small bowl, and stir into the cherry juice. Cook the sauce, stirring constantly, until the mixture thickens. Stir in the cherries and sugar and bring the mixture back to the boil. Serve with the venison.

Serves 4–6

2–2.5kg/4½–5½lb venison
    tenderloin
25g/1oz/2 tbsp butter, softened
250ml/8fl oz/1 cup water
salt and ground black pepper

For the cherry sauce
250ml/8fl oz/1 cup cherry juice
120ml/4fl oz/½ cup water
25ml/1½ tbsp cornflour (cornstarch)
425g/15oz canned or frozen
    unsweetened stoned (pitted)
    cherries
90g/3½oz/½ cup sugar

Served mainly in autumn or winter during the hunting season, venison's rich flavour and earthy taste have led to a revival in its popularity. Creamed parsnips go well with this dish together with some braised leeks and roast potatoes.

Roast Chicken with Lingonberries
Stegt Kylling med Tyttebærsovs

Serves 6–8

1 roasting chicken, about
   1.6–2kg/3½–4½lb
½ lemon
60ml/4 tbsp chopped parsley
65g/2½oz/5 tbsp butter, softened
250ml/8fl oz/1 cup chicken stock or
   water
350g/12oz/1½ cups unsweetened
   lingonberries
100–150g/3¾–5oz/½–¾ cup
   caster (superfine) sugar, to taste
salt and white pepper
potato salad, to serve

1 Preheat the oven to 220°C/425°F/Gas 7. Rinse the chicken and pat dry inside and out with kitchen paper. Rub with lemon and season.

2 Mix together the parsley and 40g/1½oz/3 tbsp of the butter and spread this inside the chicken. Close the opening with a skewer or fine string. Pour half the chicken stock or water into a roasting pan and place the chicken, breast side up, on a rack in the pan. Melt the remaining butter and brush half of it over the chicken. Roast for 30 minutes.

3 Lower the oven temperature to 180°C/350°F/Gas 4. Pour the remaining stock or water into the pan. Baste the chicken with the pan juices and the remaining melted butter and continue to cook for a further 30–40 minutes, until the juices run clear when the thickest part of the thigh is pierced. Remove from the oven, cover and leave to cool. Refrigerate the cooled chicken until ready to slice for serving.

4 Place the lingonberries in a bowl. Add the sugar a little at a time, stirring until the sugar thoroughly dissolves and the fruit is mashed. Add more sugar to taste and chill the lingonberries until ready to serve.

5 Remove the chicken from the refrigerator half an hour before serving. Just before you are ready to eat, carve the chicken and arrange the slices, together with the whole legs and wings on a serving platter. Serve with a potato salad and the lingonberry sauce.

Traditional Sunday dinner in Denmark often features sliced, roast chicken served cold with potato salad, and a sauce of tart-sweet lingonberries or cowberries, a meal that's easy on the cook. Look for frozen, unsweetened lingonberries, which are easy to sweeten to taste.

Red Berry Soup with Cream Rødgrød med Fløde

Serves 6

400g/14oz redcurrants
450g/1lb raspberries
100–150g/3¾–5oz/½–¾ cup sugar
  (depending on the sweetness of
  the fruit)
550ml/18fl oz/2½ cups blackcurrant
  juice
45ml/3 tbsp cornflour (cornstarch)
250ml/8fl oz/1 cup double (heavy)
  cream
10ml/2 tsp vanilla sugar
raspberries, to decorate

Some call this ruby-red berry soup Denmark's national dessert. Utterly simple to prepare, it can be made using a blend of various red berries. Currants and raspberries are the traditional combination, but raspberries, strawberries, blackcurrants or cherries are also delightful. Serve cold with a swirl of cream in each bowl.

1 Put the berries, sugar and 500ml/17fl oz/generous 2 cups of the blackcurrant juice into a pan and add 750ml/1¼ pints/3 cups water. Bring the mixture to the boil and cook over a medium-high heat for 3 minutes. Pour the fruit and juice through a strainer set over a pan. Use a wooden spoon to press through as much berry juice as possible.

2 In a small bowl, mix the cornflour with the remaining blackcurrant juice. Stir the cornflour mixture into the berry juice. Place the pan over a medium heat and gently bring the juice to the boil, stirring, until it thickens slightly.

3 Pour the cream into a bowl and stir in the vanilla sugar. Pour the soup into individual bowls and spoon 30ml/2 tbsp cream into each bowl, swirling it slightly. Sprinkle each bowl with a few raspberries and serve.

National Day Dessert Grundlovsdessert

Serves 6

675g/1½lb rhubarb, cut into
   2.5cm/1in pieces
115g/4oz/½ cup caster (superfine)
   sugar
30ml/2 tbsp fresh lemon juice
250ml/8fl oz/1 cup water
250ml/8fl oz/1 cup milk
1 vanilla pod (bean)
30ml/2 tbsp powdered gelatine
4 eggs, separated
1 drop red food colouring
250ml/8fl oz/1 cup double (heavy)
   cream
flaked (sliced) almonds, to decorate

1 Place the rhubarb, half the sugar, the lemon juice and the water in a pan. Bring to the boil, then simmer until the rhubarb softens.

2 Pour the milk into a pan. Slit open the vanilla pod and scrape the seeds into the milk; add the vanilla pod. Bring the milk to the boil, reduce the heat and simmer for 2 minutes. Remove from the heat to cool, and discard the vanilla pod. Soften the gelatine in 30ml/2 tbsp cold water, then pour on 120ml/4fl oz/½ cup boiling water and stir until dissolved.

3 Combine the egg yolks with the remaining sugar, and beat until light and thick. Stir the gelatine mixture into the egg yolks with the vanilla-flavoured milk and leave to thicken. Beat the egg whites into stiff peaks and fold gently into the egg yolk and milk mixture. Add a drop of red food colouring and blend until the pudding is coloured pale pink.

4 Beat the cream until stiff, and fold half into the egg mixture. Divide the rhubarb among six bowls and spoon over the pudding. Top with whipped cream and sprinkle with almonds. Chill until ready to serve.

This frothy pink pudding celebrates Denmark's National Day, which commemorates the change from a constitutional monarchy to a parliamentary democracy when King Frederick IX signed the new Constitution on 5 June 1953.

Almond Ring Cake Kransekage

1 Preheat the oven to 200°C/400°F/Gas 6. If using *kransekage* tins (pans), grease 16–18 tins. If you are not using tins, line two baking sheets with baking parchment. Draw a 17cm/6½in diameter circle on the paper. Draw circles in decreasing sizes, each 1 cm/½ in smaller than the last, ending with a 5cm/2in circle.

2 To make the cake, combine all the ground almonds with the sugar in a large pan. Add the unbeaten egg white and mix into a firm dough. Place the pan over a low heat and beat with a spoon until the dough feels hot to the touch.

3 Roll out the dough into sausages about 1cm/½in in diameter and fit them into the prepared tins. Press the overlapping ends together to make a smooth circle. Roll the dough into sausages and fit one into each circle, piecing them together as necessary. Bake the rings in the preheated oven for about 8 minutes, until the tops are a light golden brown. Remove from the oven and leave to cool in the tins.

4 To make the icing, beat the egg white until stiff, then stir in the icing sugar with the salt. Continue beating until the mixture is soft. Stir in the cream, and beat for 1 minute. Pour the icing into a piping (pastry) bag fitted with a 1.5mm/¹⁄₁₆in nozzle.

5 To assemble the cake, place the largest ring on a serving plate. Stack the remaining rings on top of one another with the smallest on top, adding a covering of icing each time, piped on in a swirling, looping pattern. Finish with a final swirl of icing, and then decorate the cake with little Danish flags, if you wish.

Unique to the baking traditions of Denmark and Norway, towers assembled from stacked rings of marzipan cake are served at festive occasions, and at special "round" birthdays at the start of a new decade.

Serves 24
For the cake
250g/9oz/2½ cups blanched
  almonds, finely ground
250g/9oz/2½ cups almonds with
  skins on, finely ground
500g/1¼lb/4½ cups icing
  (confectioners') sugar, sifted
3 egg whites

For the icing
1 egg white
175g/6oz/1½ cups icing
  (confectioners') sugar, sifted
pinch of salt
5ml/1 tsp double (heavy) cream

COOK'S TIP
Special sets of ring cake tins, 15 to 18 to a set, are often used to make the cake, but if these aren't available, the dough can be rolled by hand and looped into rings.

Plum Cake Blommerkage

1 Place the chopped plums in a pan and add the water. Bring to the boil and cook for 10–15 minutes, until soft. Set aside to cool. You will need 350ml/12fl oz/1½ cups stewed plums for the cake.

2 Preheat the oven to 180°C/350°F/Gas 4. Grease and flour a 24cm/9½ in springform cake tin (pan). Cream the butter with the sugar in a mixing bowl until light and fluffy. Beat in the eggs, one at a time. Stir in the stewed plums and the almonds. Add the bicarbonate of soda, baking powder, cardamom and salt and stir until blended. Gradually stir in the flour, a few spoons at a time, and mix until blended.

3 Pour the mixture into the prepared tin. Place 15 plum halves around the circumference of the cake and the remaining three halves in the centre, cut sides down. Sprinkle the pearl sugar over the cake. Bake for 1 hour, or until the top springs back when lightly touched. Cool in the tin for 15 minutes before unfastening the ring.

4 Beat the double cream until soft peaks form. Stir in the vanilla sugar and the icing sugar and beat until thick. Serve the cake, still slightly warm, or at room temperature, in slices topped with whipped cream.

Seasonal cooking is an obvious necessity in countries of the far north with fierce extremes of climate. Traditionally, you ate what you could grow and stored food carefully to survive until the next harvest. Fruit trees were especially prized and apple, pear and plum trees still thrive in many areas of Scandinavia. These fruits are treasured in Danish cooking, adding sweetness, texture and variety to many dishes. This cardamom-accented cake has an intriguing pale bluish-green hue from the plum skins.

Serves 10

450g/1lb stoned (pitted) fresh plums, coarsely chopped, plus 9 extra plums, stoned and halved, to decorate
300ml/½ pint/1¼ cups water
115g/4oz/½ cup unsalted (sweet) butter, softened
200g/7oz/1 cup caster (superfine) sugar
3 eggs
90g/3½oz/¾ cup toasted, finely chopped almonds
5ml/1 tsp bicarbonate of soda (baking soda)
7.5ml/1½ tsp baking powder
5ml/1 tsp ground cardamom
1.5ml/¼ tsp salt
250g/9oz/2¼ cups plain (all-purpose) flour
15ml/1 tbsp pearl sugar, to decorate
250ml/8fl oz/1 cup double (heavy) cream
10ml/2 tsp vanilla sugar
10ml/2 tsp icing (confectioners') sugar

Lenten Buns with Vanilla Cream
Fastelavnsboller

Makes 24

For the buns
50ml/2fl oz/¼ cup tepid water
40g/1½oz fresh yeast
175g/6oz/¾ cup unsalted (sweet)
    butter, softened
50g/2oz/¼ cup caster (superfine)
    sugar
2 eggs, plus 1 extra yolk
175ml/6fl oz/¾ cup milk
400g/14oz/3½ cups bread flour

For the vanilla cream filling
3 egg yolks
45ml/3 tbsp caster (superfine) sugar
10ml/2 tsp vanilla sugar
15ml/1 tbsp cornflour (cornstarch)
475ml/16fl oz/2 cups milk
pinch of salt

For the icing
1 egg white
150g/5oz/1¼ cups icing
    (confectioner's) sugar, sifted
25g/1oz/¼ cup unsweetened cocoa
    powder, sifted
pinch of salt
5ml/1 tsp double (heavy) cream
30ml/2 tbsp pearl sugar, to decorate

1 Pour the tepid water into a bowl and stir in the yeast until dissolved. Combine the butter and sugar and beat until light and fluffy. Beat in one whole egg and the extra yolk. Briefly warm the milk, add the yeast mixture and stir into the butter mixture. Stir in the flour, a little at a time, and mix to a soft dough, adding more flour if necessary.

2 Turn the dough out on to a lightly floured surface and knead until smooth. Lightly oil a large bowl. Place the dough in the bowl, cover with a towel, and leave in a warm place until doubled in size, about 1 hour.

3 To make the filling, whisk together the egg yolks and sugar in a pan. Whisk in the vanilla sugar, cornflour and milk. Add the salt. Cook over a low heat, stirring constantly, until the mixture thickens. Leave to cool.

4 Lightly grease two baking sheets. Turn the dough out on to a floured surface and divide into four. Cut each part into six pieces and shape into balls. Place on the baking sheets. Make a well in the centre of each roll, and fill with a spoonful of the cream filling. Cover with clear film (plastic wrap) and leave in a warm place for 1½–2 hours.

5 Preheat the oven to 220°C/425°F/Gas 7. Lightly beat the remaining egg and brush it over the buns. Bake for 12–15 minutes, until golden. Cool on a wire rack.

6 To make the icing, beat the egg white until stiff. Stir in the icing sugar, cocoa and salt and beat until soft. Stir in the cream and beat for 1 minute. Place a blob of icing over each bun and sprinkle with pearl sugar.

Though very few Danes still observe the Lenten fast, the holiday survives as a festive, carnival-like occasion. Traditional treats include these plump, yeasty buns, with a cream filling and various toppings.

Vanilla Rings Vanillekranse

Makes 72

400g/14oz/1¾ cup butter
130g/4½oz/⅔ cup caster (superfine)
   sugar
1 egg
1 vanilla pod (bean), finely chopped,
   or 10ml/2 tsp vanilla extract
450g/1lb/4 cups plain (all-purpose)
   flour
5ml/1 tsp baking powder
115g/4oz/1 cup blanched almonds,
   finely chopped

1 Preheat the oven to 180°C/350°F/Gas 4. Lightly grease two baking sheets.

2 Place the butter and sugar in a large bowl and beat until light and fluffy. Beat in the egg, then the chopped vanilla pod or vanilla extract.

3 Gradually stir the flour, baking powder and almonds into the creamed mixture to form a soft dough. Turn out on to a lightly floured surface and knead lightly until the dough is smooth.

4 Using a star piping nozzle or cookie press, form 5cm/2in diameter rings on the prepared baking sheets. Bake the biscuits for 8–9 minutes, until golden brown. Cool on a wire rack and store in an airtight container.

Blessed with fine ingredients, Danish pastry chefs and home cooks are renowned for creating artistically shaped and richly flavoured biscuits and cookies. For special occasions and family gatherings, no Danish table would be complete without an assortment of biscuits. These rich, buttery rings are a special favourite with children at Christmas.

Nutritional notes

Yellow Pea Soup with Horseradish Cream: Energy 248kcal/1051kJ; Protein 21.6g; Carbohydrate 32.8g, of which sugars 5.3g; Fat 4.3g, of which saturates 1.2g; Cholesterol 9mg; Calcium 69mg; Fibre 7.4g; Sodium 348mg.

Liver Pâté: Energy 366kcal/1514kJ; Protein 13.3g; Carbohydrate 1.2g, of which sugars 1g; Fat 34.3g, of which saturates 14.9g; Cholesterol 214mg; Calcium 33mg; Fibre 0.1g; Sodium 126mg.

Pickled Herring: Energy 231kcal/963kJ; Protein 12.5g; Carbohydrate 7.5g, of which sugars 7.5g; Fat 16.6g, of which saturates 1.2g; Cholesterol 32mg; Calcium 10mg; Fibre 0g; Sodium 623mg.

Danish Caviar with Toast and Crème Fraîche: Energy 208kcal/869kJ; Protein 6.5g; Carbohydrate 19.5g, of which sugars 1.8g; Fat 12.1g, of which saturates 7g; Cholesterol 99mg; Calcium 60mg; Fibre 0.6g; Sodium 731mg.

Jerusalem Artichokes au Gratin: Energy 296kcal/1230kJ; Protein 6.9g; Carbohydrate 27.6g, of which sugars 15.5g; Fat 18.1g, of which saturates 11.1g; Cholesterol 52mg; Calcium 186mg; Fibre 4.4g; Sodium 240mg.

Braised Red Cabbage: Energy 90kcal/381kJ; Protein 3.1g; Carbohydrate 19.4g, of which sugars 18g; Fat 0.5g, of which saturates 0g; Cholesterol 0mg; Calcium 98mg; Fibre 5g; Sodium 14mg.

Cucumber Salad: Energy 30kcal/125kJ; Protein 0.7g; Carbohydrate 1.1g, of which sugars 1g; Fat 2.6g, of which saturates 1.6g; Cholesterol 8mg; Calcium 26mg; Fibre 0.4g; Sodium 8mg.

Marinated Herring in Sour Cream: Energy 346kcal/1437kJ; Protein 13.5g; Carbohydrate 15.4g, of which sugars 9.7g; Fat 25.9g, of which saturates 12.5g; Cholesterol 165mg; Calcium 114mg; Fibre 1.6g; Sodium 506mg.

Smoked Salmon with Dill and Lemon: Energy 249kcal/1037kJ; Protein 9.3g; Carbohydrate 15.7g, of which sugars 8.9g; Fat 17g, of which saturates 6.2g; Cholesterol 30mg; Calcium 44mg; Fibre 0.3g; Sodium 1265mg.

Prawns with Egg and Cucumber: Energy 256kcal/1066kJ; Protein 17.6g; Carbohydrate 6.4g, of which sugars 0.5g; Fat 18.1g, of which saturates 5.5g; Cholesterol 264mg; Calcium 90mg; Fibre 0.2g; Sodium 337mg.

The Veterinarian's Evening Sandwich: Energy 373kcal/1545kJ; Protein 16.1g; Carbohydrate 8.1g, of which sugars 1.9g; Fat 30.9g, of which saturates 10.8g; Cholesterol 158mg; Calcium 33mg; Fibre 0.9g; Sodium 1019mg.

Pork Fillet with Crispy Onion Rings: Energy 460kcal/1911kJ; Protein 24.5g; Carbohydrate 20.1g, of which sugars 3.9g; Fat 31.8g, of which saturates 7.5g; Cholesterol 82mg; Calcium 50mg; Fibre 1.8g; Sodium 218mg.

Beef Tartare with Egg Yolk, Onion and Beetroot: Energy 291kcal/1215kJ; Protein 22.1g; Carbohydrate 11g, of which sugars 4.8g; Fat 18g, of which saturates 7.7g; Cholesterol 258mg; Calcium 56mg; Fibre 1.8g; Sodium 201mg.

Salt Cod with Mustard Sauce: Energy 570kcal/2387kJ; Protein 70.6g; Carbohydrate 8.8g, of which sugars 8.4g; Fat 28.4g, of which saturates 10.5g; Cholesterol 296mg; Calcium 86mg; Fibre 0g; Sodium 1592mg.

Fish Cakes: Energy 407kcal/1700kJ; Protein 48.5g; Carbohydrate 5.5g, of which sugars 0.6g; Fat 21.4g, of which saturates 7.9g; Cholesterol 259mg; Calcium 64mg; Fibre 0.3g; Sodium 1029mg.

Fried Salt Herring with Red Onion Compote: Energy 672kcal/2805kJ; Protein 35.9g; Carbohydrate 43.5g, of which sugars 23.7g; Fat 34.1g, of which saturates 12.3g; Cholesterol 114mg; Calcium 186mg; Fibre 2.8g; Sodium 460mg.

Roast Pork, Crackling and Glazed Potatoes: Energy 654kcal/2735kJ; Protein 36.9g; Carbohydrate 39.5g, of which sugars 26.2g; Fat 39.9g, of which saturates 16.1g; Cholesterol 124mg; Calcium 36mg; Fibre 1.5g; Sodium 152mg.

Danish Meatballs: Energy 404kcal/1683kJ; Protein 28.4g; Carbohydrate 8.7g, of which sugars 3.8g; Fat 28.8g, of which saturates 14.9g; Cholesterol 211mg; Calcium 112mg; Fibre 0.3g; Sodium 307mg.

Beef Patties with Onions and Fried Egg: Energy 527kcal/2189kJ; Protein 32.7g; Carbohydrate 11.8g, of which sugars 2.9g; Fat 39.3g, of which saturates 18.5g; Cholesterol 342mg; Calcium 104mg; Fibre 0.5g; Sodium 375mg.

Venison Tenderloins with Cherry Sauce: Energy 518kcal/2197kJ; Protein 74.6g; Carbohydrate 37.5g, of which sugars 33.7g; Fat 10.8g, of which saturates 4.8g; Cholesterol 176mg; Calcium 45mg; Fibre 0.4g; Sodium 220mg.

Roast Chicken with Lingonberries: Energy 405kcal/1682kJ; Protein 24.9g; Carbohydrate 15.3g, of which sugars 15.3g; Fat 27.4g, of which saturates 10.2g; Cholesterol 145mg; Calcium 36mg; Fibre 1.4g; Sodium 151mg.

Red Berry Soup with Cream: Energy 383kcal/1606kJ; Protein 3.1g; Carbohydrate 44g, of which sugars 37.1g; Fat 23g, of which saturates 14.1g; Cholesterol 57mg; Calcium 84mg; Fibre 3.6g; Sodium 25mg.

National Day Dessert: Energy 375kcal/1566kJ; Protein 11.6g; Carbohydrate 23.6g, of which sugars 23.6g; Fat 26.9g, of which saturates 15.4g; Cholesterol 186mg; Calcium 204mg; Fibre 1.6g; Sodium 78mg.

Almond Ring Cake: Energy 241kcal/1013kJ; Protein 5g; Carbohydrate 30.8g, of which sugars 30.3g; Fat 11.7g, of which saturates 1g; Cholesterol 0mg; Calcium 65mg; Fibre 1.5g; Sodium 15mg.

Plum Cake: Energy 311kcal/1308kJ; Protein 6.4g; Carbohydrate 44.5g, of which sugars 15.9g; Fat 13.2g, of which saturates 7.4g; Cholesterol 89mg; Calcium 86mg; Fibre 2.4g; Sodium 102mg.

Lenten Buns with Vanilla Cream: Energy 186kcal/782kJ; Protein 3.9g; Carbohydrate 25.6g, of which sugars 12.2g; Fat 8.3g, of which saturates 4.6g; Cholesterol 67mg; Calcium 70mg; Fibre 0.6g; Sodium 77mg.

Vanilla Rings: Energy 78kcal/326kJ; Protein 1g; Carbohydrate 6.3g, of which sugars 2.1g; Fat 5.6g, of which saturates 3g; Cholesterol 14mg; Calcium 14mg; Fibre 0.3g; Sodium 35mg.

Index